I0817047

MEDITATIONS
ON
DEATH

MEDITATIONS ON DEATH

PREPARING FOR ETERNITY

THOMAS À KEMPIS

Translated by
FR. ROBERT NIXON, OSB

TAN Books
Gastonia, North Carolina

Translated by Fr. Robert Nixon, OSB

Cover design by Andrew Schmalen

Cover image credit: Saint Francis in Meditation, Michelangelo Merisi da Caravaggio, oil on canvas, Gallerie Nazionali Barberini / Bridgeman Images.

Interior image credits: Gustave Dore Bible: The Last Judgement, Gustave Dore, engraving, © Look and Learn / Bridgeman Images (xvi), Revelation: Vision of Death, Gustave Dore, engraving, Lebrecht History / Bridgeman Images (30), The Divine Comedy, Gustave Dore, engraving, Stefano Bianchetti / Bridgeman Images (62).

ISBN: 978-1-5051-2806-2
Kindle ISBN: 978-1-5051-2807-9
ePUB ISBN: 978-1-5051-2808-6

Published in the United States by
TAN Books
PO Box 269
Gastonia, NC 28053
www.TANBooks.com

Printed in India

"Man is like to vanity: his days pass away like a shadow."

—Psalm 143:4

Contents

Part III: Canticles to Heaven

Translator's Note

A popular and venerable saying, variously attributed to Socrates, Plato, and Cicero, asserts that "the whole of the life of the wise person should be a preparation for death." This principle, if evident even to the pagan sages of antiquity, is of greater pertinence to those enlightened by the truth of the Gospel. For if an eternity of either ineffable bliss or of horrendous torment awaits each soul after its departure from this world, then our preparation for this departure is quite literally the most important duty of our present life. And, whereas all else in life is inherently uncertain, death is an unalterable and inescapable reality which each human being must sooner or later face.

Throughout the entire tradition of Christian spirituality, the contemplation of death has been a virtually ubiquitous practice, and it is universally recommended by the saints and Doctors of the Church. As one example among many, Saint Benedict, the patriarch of all monks of the West, wisely counsels the spiritual seeker to "keep death daily before your eyes."[1] For nothing else is more efficacious in moderating our earthly desires, in promoting awareness of the eternal destiny of the immortal soul, and in imparting courage and consolation in the face of adversity and tribulation. For it is mindfulness of death alone which puts our mortal life into its proper perspective.

The practice of meditation on death assumed particular prominence in late-medieval spirituality (that is to say, in the fourteenth and fifteenth centuries). The reasons for this were many—including the multitude of calamities (such as war, plague, and famine) which afflicted Europe at the time, the rapid rate of social change and the prevailing political instability. Also included is the rediscovery and popular circulation of the writings of the ancient philosophers, especially Plato, Cicero, Seneca, and Marcus Aurelius.

The greatest and most representative spiritual writer of this rich and complex era was arguably Thomas à Kempis (1380–1470), best known as the author of the ever-popular classic *The Imitation of Christ.* Thomas, who was of humble birth, commenced his religious life in the Brotherhood of Common Life, an association of men

---

1 *Rule of Saint Benedict, 4:47.*

(primarily students and scholars) who lived a kind of quasi-monastic life in community, without being bound by permanent vows. Following this, he entered the Canons Regular, and he was ordained a priest after completing the necessary course of studies and formation.

Thomas was an avid copyist of manuscripts, reproducing by hand the entire Bible no less than four times, as well as copying the complete works of Saint Bernard of Clairvaux, and many others. He was also an extraordinarily prolific author, and his works (which span several weighty volumes in the multitude of editions of them which have appeared) encompass the genres of spiritual and moral treatises, homilies, didactic works, hagiography, and poetry. Despite the immense popularity of *The Imitation of Christ*, many of his wonderful writings remain untranslated to this day.

This volume contains a short but extremely powerful work attributed to Thomas à Kempis, offering a moving, profound, and vivid meditation upon death and the "Four Last Things" (i.e., the event of death itself, the Final Judgment, the torments of hell, and the happiness of heaven). The present English rendering is a translation from the Latin text of the 1523 Paris edition, published by Jocodus Badius Ascensius of the *Opera Thomae a Campis* (*Works of Thomas à Kempis*).

It is to be noted that the attribution to Thomas is not entirely certain. This uncertainty of attribution is not at all surprising when one considers that Thomas generally preferred, out of his characteristic humility, to circulate his works anonymously. Indeed, even most of the early manuscript copies of the *Imitation of Christ* itself do not indicate any author.[2]

Nevertheless, these *Meditations on Death* are entirely consistent with the focus on eschatological and ultimate realities to be found in Thomas's writings and other authors of the period. If Thomas did not write them, then they are certainly the product of someone of the same era, and imbued with the same passionate but down-to-earth approach to the spiritual life.

The two brief poetic interludes, or canticles, which appear in part III are translations of excerpts from the *Cantica Spirituala* (*Spiritual Canticles*) of Thomas, a collection of short spiritual poems or songs. These works appear in virtually all of the editions of the collected works of Thomas (including the 1523 edition noted above) and are certainly his authentic works but have never before appeared in English. The versions offered

---

2 It is interesting to note that in the current Roman Breviary, the readings taken from the *Imitation of Christ* do not name any author for the work.

here emulate the regular rhyme schemes of the original Latin texts and, for this reason, exercise a considerable degree of literary freedom. The translator hopes that any shortcomings or deficiencies in these will be attributed entirely to himself, but whatever is found to be meritorious and edifying may be credited to Thomas.

For many contemporary readers, the idea of a booklet[3] of *Meditations on Death* may well seem slightly morbid, macabre, or even depressing. But this is not truly the case at all. For death is an essential part of life, and the contemplation of death is, in fact, simply an honest recognition of the finitude of our own mortal condition. It is only through coming to terms with the reality and inevitability of death in time that we can come to appreciate the true significance and value of life in eternity. The relationship between life and death may seem paradoxical or contradictory, yet it is necessary and essential.

In our contemporary culture, there is often a tendency to conceal or deny the reality of human mortality. Yet this "death-denying" culture is, ironically, also one that often systematically denies life itself, through

[3] Thomas à Kempis intended his works to be read as such since he uses the term "Libellus,"or "small book." Like many writers of the period, he generally divides his texts into short, readily digestible chapters.

practices such as contraception, abortion, euthanasia, and same-sex marriage.

Sacred Scripture tells us that "if we die with Christ, we shall also live with Him. If we suffer with Him, we shall also reign with Him."[4] May the courageous and humble contemplation of death help us to shun sin and to cultivate virtue; may it help us overcome the temptations and allurements of that which is passing and ephemeral and help to strive instead for that which is eternal; and may it empower us to "seize the day"—both by making the most of our earthly lives and by yearning constantly for the beatitude of heaven, the glory and splendor which "eye has not seen, nor ear heard, nor the human heart conceived."[5]

May the Blessed Virgin Mary, her most chaste spouse Saint Joseph (the patron saint of the dying), and all the holy angels and saints assist us in this endeavor through their unfailing intercession, guidance, and example.

Fr. Robert Nixon, OSB
Abbey of the Most Holy Trinity
New Norcia, Western Australia

---

4 2 Timothy 2:11–12.

5 1 Corinthians 2:9.

Part I
Reflections on the Last Things

1

Consideration of One's Own Death

My friend, it is most useful for you to call to mind frequently and assiduously the reality of your own death. This, indeed, is the one universal reality of our human condition—for in this life, some are rich while others are poor, some are masters while others are servants, some learned while others are simple, and some are blessed by happiness and good fortune while others are struck down by misfortune and calamity. Yet all face death with equal certainty. And though death itself is a certainty, its time and manner of arrival are profoundly uncertain.

So consider firstly the uncertainty of the year, month, day, and hour of your death. Death often arrives with no or little warning, coming like a thief in the night or descending upon us unexpectedly, like a falcon swooping upon a hapless dove. Often it arrives on the occasion you least expect it, and at the time when you are least prepared for it. Very often death comes to a person when he still expects to have much longer to live and looks forward to an abundance of time in which to repent for his sins, to amend his vices, and to improve his life and conduct.

My advice, therefore, is to live as if you could die at any moment and to live each day as if it could be your last. And be mindful that this is no idle or hypothetical speculation or a mere morally edifying imagining but a frighteningly real and imminent possibility at all times! In fact, it is not a possibility only, but it is a *certainty.* For while everything else in the future course of your life—your success or failure, your prosperity or poverty, your happiness or wretchedness—are unknown, hidden, and indeterminate, *death* is the one thing of which you may be absolutely sure.

Consider also, the severe weakness and debility which often precedes the actual event of death. This debility and weakness is truly nothing other than a herald of our mortality and the oblivion which will engulf our earthly being. The period of severe illness which precedes death for many is not, indeed, the ideal time for repentance.

Apart from its extreme uncertainty of duration, it is generally a time when the spirit and the mind are gravely weakened and strong resolutions have become virtually impossible. And if one is confined to bed, genuine emendation of one's life is hardly meaningfully possible at all. For the person confined to bed and in the throes of physical and spiritual dissolution can hardly undertake any real works of piety or penance.

Thus "deathbed repentance" is inherently uncertain in its efficacy since its sincerity is not demonstrated or supported by any works or reformation of life. It *may* be efficacious in some instances, but it cannot be relied upon since not even the person concerned can be certain of the genuineness of their contrition.

Consider next your own self in your dying moments, and reflect upon the stains on your conscience, your unatoned sins, and your unamended vices. These will all flood into your heart as a bitter torrent at that fateful time, like a river of regret or a stream of sorrow. And each unatoned crime and unconfessed sin will painfully prick your heart, like a sharp and uncomfortable thorn. How much you will then long for another year of life and health, or even another day or another hour, in which to atone and amend yourself!

O mortal, reflect carefully upon that unknown time when you will come to your final hour, and when the lethal hand of death will fall upon your shoulder, and when you will be compelled to cross that dark stream from which none have ever returned! When you enter into the realm of eternity, your whole past life will seem like a mere moment and appear to be like an insubstantial dream from which you are now awakening. Reflect upon the immense pain and torments which await so very many (countless multitudes, in fact), and often all for the sake of some passing, momentary pleasure, be it the gratification of the physical senses or the appeasement of pride and vanity. Reflect also upon the infinite joys and blessedness which those condemned will have lost forever. This irreparable and infinite loss is, indeed, perhaps more severe an affliction than any of the other torments which could be imagined.

Consider also how bitter will be the separation from all those you love, and the extreme and everlasting dishonor of eternal condemnation. In this world, human beings make enormous efforts to acquire honor for themselves and seek avidly to attain happiness in any form possible. Yet how few make any comparable effort to attain the glory which lasts forever and to secure for themselves the happiness which never ends!

Think also about the fate of your earthly body, this lump of clay out of which has been formed by the hand of God. For indeed it shall rot and decay, and grow black and putrid, withering away to nothing and eventually crumbling to dust. And at the point of death, a multitude of demons will appear before you, ready to seize upon each departed soul. With gaping jaws and grasping hands, these shall be like "roaring lions seeking whom they may devour."[1]

Next, consider how the condemned soul must pass to a region entirely unknown to it, where a multitude of cruel and vicious demons shall viciously await it. It shall then long to return to its body. But it will be entirely unable, for all the windows and portals of entrance and exit thereto are now forever closed. Yes, an unpassable abyss lies between the realms of the living and the dead!

Instead, the condemned soul will find itself in an immense cavern of utter and impenetrable darkness, fetid and heavy with all the charnel odors of the grave. And the various evil spirits of each of the vices shall seek it out to torment it. Thus the spirit of pride shall hunt down those who were proud during their lifetime, and

---

[1] See 1 Peter 5:8.

the spirit of lust shall seize upon those who were lustful. And so it will be for vices of every kind, each vice having its own particular tormenting spirits. And the nature of these tormenting spirits will correspond to the vice which they punish. Thus, the infernal spirit which punishes pride shall constantly mock and humiliate its victims, whereas the demon which punishes sloth will compel them to undertake incessant, arduous, and unending labor.

Finally, consider how after the moment of death, you shall have to stand before that most awesome tribunal of judgment to await your eternal sentence. This final sentence, once pronounced by the immortal Judge, can never, ever be revoked or changed. For indeed, it is written in Holy Scripture that "wherever the tree falls, there it will lie."[2]

Consider also how your mortal body, upon which you have bestowed such care and love whilst you lived, will be enclosed in a cold and soon-to-be-forgotten tomb. Your very self will be consigned to perpetual oblivion, at least as far as this world is concerned. You will be just like a guest who has visited for one day and then left, and whom no one remembers![3]

---

2 Ecclesiastes 11:3.

3 See Wisdom 8:5–12.

But for those who have lived holy and upright lives, and who have prepared themselves diligently by prayer and penance, the situation will be very different indeed. For when they realize that they are about to pass from this world of sorrows, this valley of tears, they will not fear at all. On the contrary, they shall rejoice knowing that they are about to depart for their true native land of heaven, and there to enjoy unending and infinite bliss in the company of glorious angels and saints, illuminated by the magnificent and glorious radiance of the Holy Trinity Itself.

And the cause of this joy is nothing other than the fact that they carry with them the testimony of a clear and innocent conscience. Exultantly they shall ascend to the realm of everlasting happiness and peace, departing from the miseries of this present world without a single shadow of regret. For there shall be no bond of earthly concupiscence or carnal desire which enchains them to this lower realm, and they shall feel not a single pang of sorrow or regret to bid this world of time and space a final farewell.

2

The Torments of Hell

To imagine what the infernal realm of hell is really like is something which entirely exceeds the capacity of the human mind. For whatever horrors, pains, and torments we can conceive of or imagine, the reality is incomparably worse. Nevertheless, though we can never accurately describe it in words or depict it in comprehensible images, it is useful to bring to mind certain visions which the saints have recorded in their writings and discourses. For by means of such visions, they have been granted genuine insights, albeit by means of similitudes, into this dreadful reality. And such insights serve as a profitable warning and admonition to all the living.

Summon up before the eye of your mind, therefore, a horrible and swirling chaos, or a lightless and sinister subterranean cavern, fuming with every kind of unspeakable foulness and swarming with hideous phantasms, or a burning and bottomless pit, completely suffused with scorching, acrid, and inextinguishable fires.

Alternatively, you may imagine a great and immense city populated entirely by the damned and by devils, where the atmosphere is permeated by an invisible, black fire. This invisible but all-pervading fire burns with a searing intensity but emits no light or luminescence whatsoever. And over this infernal metropolis—which is the capital of hell—there is an unfathomable, opaque darkness, whereby both the senses and the mind are suffocated and reduced to a state of perpetual, tormented confusion. The air there is filled with the dire resonance of the ceaseless groans, laments, squeals, and wailings of the inhabitants. For all of the damned souls cry out in pain and despair over the varied tortures and miseries they endure, while the demons (whose role it is to torment those condemned) issue forth their own malevolent cacophony of cruel taunts, callous derision, and sinister, diabolical laughter.

And each of the tortures and miseries experienced by those who populate hell are unique and particular to each individual. For this reason, each lost soul (despite the countless multitude of such souls in this city) abide in a state of utter isolation, bereft of all companionship and consolation. Yet, on the other hand, all the varied and multifarious torments and agonies are also one and the same—partaking in the common and unspeakable pain of everlasting damnation, which is nothing other than eternal separation from the Supreme Good of the divine love and glory of God.

Consider next the bitterness and extremity of the pains which are suffered there. These far exceed any pains which our bodies or hearts can experience during this mortal life. For the fire which burns so ceaselessly there is incomparably hotter than any flame found here on earth. Indeed, it is said that the fire of hell exceeds the heat of earthly fire to the same extent that our earthly fire is hotter than a mere painted picture of fire.

Next, consider the freezing cold which prevails in hell. You might wonder how this coldness can be possible, given the omnipresence of the searing flames. But the dire chill of hell is, paradoxically, felt at the very same time as its scorching fires. It is true that the pain and discomfort caused by this malevolent and diabolic combination of burning heat and bitter cold cannot be imagined by the mortal mind. Perhaps the closest approximation to be found in our earthly realms is the ghastly feeling of those afflicted with virulent and noxious fevers, who experience an overwhelming heat and a chilling frigidity at the same time, and hence they simultaneously sweat profusely whilst shivering violently.

Yet one can gain a sense of the horrid extremity of this condition by the sounds which fill the air in the accursed city of hell. For there resounds an unremitting cacophony of the grinding of teeth and gnashing of jaws, and wailing and weeping, and groaning and grunting, and crying and cursing. For in the delirium of their despair, the tormented souls continually utter the most disgusting blasphemies and imprecations against God Himself—the same God from whom their own wickedness has separated them forevermore. And, in the same breath, they curse with the most galling vitriol the entire universe, their wretched state, and their very own selves as well.

Think, too, about the innumerable multiplicity and incalculable abundance of these pains and torments. For, as noted, there simultaneously prevails an inextinguishable fire of unbearable intensity as well as a bone-chilling, blood-freezing cold. The foulest miasmas fill the nostrils, with the charnel stench of decomposition and the tomb, and the rank fetor of a putrid swamp. And this wretched odor is of such intensity as to dizzy the mind and move the innards to nausea. And a darkness which is so dense and heavy as to be palpable enshrouds everything.

Each one of the senses—which in this earthly life so often are misused and so come to serve as the handmaids and conduits of sin—will experience torments in its own particular way. Thus the vision of each lost soul will be subjected to the sight of grotesque and gruesome demons, and scenes of appalling ugliness and horror. These will be of such hideousness as to be comparable to the ugliness of the Medusa of the ancient legends, the mere sight of which was sufficient to turn a human being into stone. And the sense of hearing will be mercilessly disturbed and pained with the discord of groans and agonized screams, as described previously.

Disgusting and nauseating odors of decomposition and death, together with the acrid stench of sulfur, will perpetually plague the nose. The sense of taste will be assaulted without remission by a stomach-turning concoction of pitch and lead mixed together, and then dissolved in vinegar and gall. This will saturate the lips and fill the mouth and throat as an invisible infusion or diabolical brew. Hence, the tormented souls will try to avoid breathing, knowing that to breathe will mean taking in the foul stench and disgusting flavor of the hellish atmosphere. But, of course, it is impossible to stop breathing by an act of will. So the damned will be in a state of continually alternating suffocation and disgust from which no rest or respite is possible.

And, finally, the sense of touch will be forever inflamed and aggravated by the acrid and searing heat of "the fire which is never extinguished" and the mordant bite of "the worm which ceaseth not to gnaw."[4] How unimaginably horrible all this will be! Merely to think of it is enough to cause the heart to shudder and the skin to grow pale.

Reflect also upon the execrable and loathsome companions you would have in hell. Firstly, there are the demons and fiends whose sole task it is to torture condemned souls. With what relentless cruelty and insatiable avidity they undertake their ghoulish and macabre work! Such is the perverseness and depravity of their nature that they take diabolic delight in inflicting the maximum amount of pain possible, in the most varied and heinous ways. Furthermore, they constantly insult and mock those whom they punish, exclaiming, "Where is all your glory and acclaim now, you vile wretch? Where is your former pride, your arrogance, and your smug and self-satisfied complacency?"

---

4 See Mark 9:48.

For these diabolical beings, though entirely wicked and evil in their own natures, know full well the power, majesty, and glory of God.[5] Therefore, as much as they are adversaries of all goodness, they nevertheless feel utter contempt and loathing for condemned sinners, who through acts of their own free will, threw away the eternal bliss offered to them.

In this realm of dire punishment and exactly measured retributions, each one will suffer in the particular limbs or members whereby they committed their sins whilst on earth. Thus those who committed sins with their hands shall feel pains in their hands, and those who committed sins with their tongues—such as gossip, or slander, or perjury—will be afflicted with torments of the tongue. And thus it shall be with each of the members of the body, from the greatest to the least. Alas, then for those whose sins are against chastity! The pains and torments which they will experience can hardly decently be described in this treatise and are therefore left to the imagination of the reader.

But despite these horrendous physical pains, the interior and spiritual sufferings of the damned will far outweigh the totality of their exterior torments. First,

5 See James 2:19. "Even the demons believe, and they tremble in terror."

a guilty conscience will gnaw continually at the heart, like the deathless worm, eating away greedily at the soul from inside. Every sin ever committed will come before the eyes of memory, for each of the damned has unbounded time to reflect upon its guilt. And the memory of these individual sins and crimes will be like painful drops of acid dripping upon the flesh.

And then there shall be also an infinite and unassuageable regret, for each of those condemned will realize that he could very easily have evaded the punishments which he now suffers. Yes, by a little self-restraint and self-denial while on earth, or by a sincere act of repentance and a little penance while he was still alive, he could readily have escaped the sentence of eternal damnation! But now, sadly, that chance has vanished forever. From the perspective of eternity, how vain, empty and deceitful will all the pleasures of sin and vice seem! For compared to the fathomless magnitude of eternity, what is our earthly life but a passing shadow, a momentary dream, a transient and unstable mist?

And how bitter will be the regret of those who refused to repent or to submit themselves to the mercy of God or to accept the truths of the holy Church, through stubbornness or pride, or foolish confidence in their own misguided intelligence or the wisdom of this world! Of what benefit will be human pride when confronted with the perpetual fires of the abyss? For then it shall bring no consolation but rather serve only to augment and sharpen the severity of the endless sufferings.

And it is not only the pangs of conscience and regret which will afflict the inmates of the inferno but also all wicked passions—for the fires of wrath and envy shall burn within them, multiplying all of their sufferings many times over. And thus shall be their melancholy and desperate lamentations, "Alas, what profit has our earthly splendor and luxury brought to us now? Where have our former riches and ranks, our praises and privileges, gone? All that has passed away, never to return! Perpetual pain has supplanted the passing pleasures of sin; eternal ignominy has replaced our hollow and inane pride. Our vainglory has vanished; our vanity has been vanquished!"

Finally, my friend, consider the sheer magnitude of the duration of these unimaginable sorrows. For they literally have no end, not even after a thousand years, or a thousand, thousand years! Not even after the number of years to which any could count in a thousand, thousand years! The years of pain shall exceed the number of stars in the sky, the centuries of sorrow will exceed the number of grains of sand on the seashore. For there is no hope of redemption or escape, and there is *no* end, none at all.

Those pains will last forever,
The torment ceasing never;
Oh, countless are the years,
And endless are the tears.

From hell there's no release,
The agonies won't cease;
Though endless ages turn,
Its flames yet still will burn!

3

The Final Judgment

My friend, reflect next upon how much terror and anxiety there will be at the great scene of the Final Judgment! The miraculous trumpets of angels shall then sound a deafening fanfare. Great bolts of blazing lightening will illuminate the earth and the sky with a blinding luminosity. Tumultuous thunder will roar, penetrating into the very depths of each human heart. The earth, the sea, and heavens themselves will all tremble!

Consider the enormity of the wrath of the most just Judge, which will blaze against those who have offended Him through disobedience and disbelief. From this wrath, an abject and paralyzing fear will engulf the minds of all those who are guilty and terrify even the innocent.

And consider the fateful and irreversible division of the assembled multitude which shall then take place. For those who are righteous, humble, and meek will be directed to the right hand of the Throne of Judgment, whereas the proud, envious, uncharitable, and wicked will be sent away to the left. Those on the right will rejoice, knowing that they are destined for eternal bliss, while those on the left will quake and quail, realizing the horrendous fate that awaits them. And none will know with certainty in advance to which side they will be sent—neither pope nor bishop, nor king, nor beggar, nor even convicted criminal. For God alone perceives into the depths of the heart and knows all secret thoughts and actions, and He shows mercy to whom He wills. Thus there will be two standing together [apparently similar in their conduct, beliefs and morals], and one will be taken away and the other left behind.[6]

How shocked and taken aback will be many of those who were proud and elated in this vain and deceptive world! For the Lord God shall exalt above such presumptuous people the poor, the wretched, the rejected, and the lowly. They will see those whom they regarded as vile and treated with contempt and disdain being

[6] See Matthew 24:40.

richly rewarded, and being granted all the dignities and splendor of heaven. The proud and haughty will then declare in their hearts, "These are the ones whom we held in derision and ridicule. We considered their lives as foolishness and believed that their ends would be without honor. But, behold, now they are numbered amongst the children of God!"[7] And then all the righteous will stand up boldly against those who mocked and persecuted them in this present life.

Consider, my friend, the account and explanation which you will be required to render for all your deeds and thoughts when you stand before that awesome tribunal of judgment. The book of your life shall be opened, which will contain a detailed record of all your actions, utterances, and desires and plans, from the moment of your birth until your final breath. And you may be questioned about *anything* at all.

Imagine the heavenly Jerusalem, situated close by the tribunal of judgment, and illuminated by an ineffable, celestial light. That holy light will shine so brightly that it will expose the very depths of every heart. Within that all-revealing luminosity will be an irrefutable witness to every single thing you have ever done, or said,

---

[7] Wisdom 5:4–5.

or thought! There will be *no* secrets, none at all. And thus sinners will stand condemned both by their own consciences and by the whole universe itself.

And Christ will display there the bloody signs of His most noble passion and the wounds which He sustained for the sake of our redemption. Consider the bitter guilt and unspeakable shame which shall then overwhelm the wicked, and the pangs of conscience which shall pierce their very hearts!

Imagine also the deafening thunder, as if resounding through every particle and atom of creation, and the irrevocable sentence which shall be uttered against the wicked: "Go forth, ye wicked, into the everlasting fires prepared for the devil and his angels." But consider also the sweet and delightful invitation which shall be extended to all the just, calling them to partake in the eternal banquet of indescribable, infinite bliss: "Come unto me, ye blessed of my Father!"[8]

Consider how, at that moment, every work of mercy and piety which you have performed during this life will be seen clearly by Christ, the eternal Judge, and that no good work shall fail to receive its due reward.

---

[8] See Matthew 25:31–46.

My friend, it is wise to call to mind this Final Judgment very frequently! Whenever you have to decide upon a course of action, reflect for a moment upon how you will account for it on that last day. Will it cause you to be ashamed or to feel regret, or to fear the retributions due to it? Or will it be counted joyfully to your credit before that omniscient tribunal? Always remember that each one of your deeds is done in the full sight of Christ and His angels, and shape your actions accordingly.

4

The Joys of Heaven

The true nature of the joys of heaven are necessarily beyond our present comprehension and surpass our thoughts, sensations, words, and desires. Nevertheless, it is both possible and helpful to *try* to imagine them, according to our limited mortal capacities. For this provides a very powerful and efficacious encouragement for the cultivation of virtue and the resistance to the temptations to sin. In meditating upon the joys of heaven, the authentic visions and similitudes which can be found amongst the writings of the saints provide a wonderful and delightful source of inspiration.

According to such visions (and to the testimony of Sacred Scripture itself), heaven may be likened to a great city miraculously constructed from the purest gold and the most precious gemstones. Each of its gates is miraculously fashioned from a single, immense pearl.[9] And that glorious, gleaming metropolis shall be adorned and surrounded by verdant and gorgeous fields, filled with multicolored flowers of incomparable and entrancing beauty. And in that city, the tranquil warmth and gentle light of spring shall prevail eternally, and the air will be suffused with fragrant perfumes offering ever-new and intoxicating delights. And the vividness of its reality shall surpass that of this present life, just as that of our current waking reality surpasses in vividness and intensity the visions of a dream.

But beyond this, consider, my friend, the infinite and unutterable joy which shall arise from the pure and direct perception of the most Holy Trinity! This is the mystic and unfathomable wonder referred to as the "beatific vision." For this Holy Trinity, mysterious and beyond all conception, is the perfect archetype and ultimate epitome of all that is beautiful, all that is good, and all that is delightful. In beholding this glorious Trinity, you will know all there is to know, and you shall possess all that your heart desires—rather, even more than your heart desires and could ever desire, and even more than your mind could ever conceive! For you will be united with the infinite beatitude, the

9 See Revelation 21.

boundless power, the infinite glory, and the perfect immortality of the Godhead itself.

Reflect, too, upon the humanity of Christ, our Savior. For our sake, He descended from His native realm of unapproachable light to assume the wretchedness of our mortal condition, to become one poor, persecuted, and despised, a "Man of sorrows and acquainted with suffering."[10] But now that He is throned at the right hand of the Father and crowned with ineffable glory, His holy humanity remains, but it is now exalted and made divine. And this humanity which the glorified Christ possesses and has made immortal, glorious, and pure is one and the same as the humanity which is your very own nature too, O Reader! And by Christ's mysterious union with human nature, your own nature shall be united with that of God.

Imagine the joy which you will derive from the wonderful company with which you will be surrounded in heaven. For there will be the glorious ever-Virgin Mary, adored by the angels, and radiant with the perfection of her immaculate, maidenly beauty! There will also be all the saints—the noble apostles, the white-robed martyrs, the chaste and graceful virgins, and the wise and

---

[10] Isaiah 53:3.

holy confessors. And the whole company of heaven—the countless multitude of holy angels and saints—will all share one and the same limitless joy. And this joy will be continually augmented by the very act of sharing it, as each will delight ecstatically in the beatitude of the other.

Your resurrected body, freed from all corruption and taint of sin and mortality, will also participate fully in the delights of this realm, no less than your soul. Immortality, impassibility, complete and unimpaired liberty and agility, and celestial beauty—all of these will be yours forever! And your mind will be enriched with all the plenitude of knowledge, righteousness, and contentment, such that it will know no disturbance or limitation or anxiety whatsoever—no, not even the shadow or memory of these shall remain.

Moreover, all of this you will enjoy with absolute and perfect security. You will no more need to flee from any temptations of sin, nor resist any impulse to sin or evil. And no foe shall ever attack you, no misfortune will ever befall you, nothing whatsoever will be able to harm you or to threaten your perfect happiness! Thus there will prevail forever uninhibited liberty, unassailable well-being, unimaginable pleasure, pure and glorious love, and splendid honor and peace.

As Saint Anselm has said, whatever you wish for, you shall immediately have, and whatever you do *not* wish for, will never befall you.

May we all, by the grace and mercy of God, attain to that most blessed state! Amen.

G. Doré
H PISA

Part II
A Discourse in the Person of a Sinner about to Die

5

Mindfulness of Death: A Sure Remedy to the Vices

Author's Prologue

My friend, whenever you are plagued by some difficulty or adversity, or tested by some temptation, or find that your enthusiasm for good works is fading or waning, or divine worship begins to seem tedious and irksome to you, there is a sure and effective remedy for you! And I shall now tell you what this secret remedy to all spiritual tepidity is.

First, sit yourself in your private room, close the door, and recollect your mind and your senses to yourself, putting aside all distraction. Then think of the day of your own death. Imagine yourself lying there on your bed, in the throes of death, perhaps laboring with some fatal illness, and knowing that your earthly life is now very quickly drawing its last moment.

My friend, contemplate the horrendous struggle which you shall sooner or later encounter! Imagine yourself upon the very point of death, about to cross that irremeable threshold into the world to come. This is an event which may not in any way be escaped whatsoever, not by anyone—it is the one certainty of our human life. And, for all you know, it may well be today that the final bell tolls for you!

Imagine to yourself what will be your thoughts and your words in those dying moments. Now, imagine the sinner about to face death. Shall his or her thoughts and words not be something very like that which follows?

[Here commences the discourse in the person of a sinner about to die]

Alas, the pains of death now surround me, streams of iniquity flow all around me, and the snares of death have trapped me![1] O my God, why was I ever born into this treacherous world, or why did I not perish the moment I was brought forth into the light of day?[2] The beginning of my life was accompanied by

[1] Psalm 18:5–6.

[2] See Job 3:11.

pain and uncertainty as I came forth from the womb struggling and crying my infant's tears, weak and utterly helpless. And now my end is likewise accompanied by sorrow and agony, by tears and regret!

O Death, how bitter is the thought of you to the sinful person?[3] Yet infinitely more bitter than this thought is your presence! Late was I to come to real belief and repentance for my sinful life; yet how rapidly I succumb to my demise and how quickly the stream of my life flows away. O Death, my final foe and last companion, you have sprung upon me suddenly. You have seized me in your chilling and inescapable grasp, like a lion waiting in ambush! With your unbreakable ropes, you have bound me, and with chains of constricting iron, you drag me after you, just as a condemned criminal is dragged off to the gallows.

I clasp my hands together and groan from the depths of my heart, longing in vain to flee from this fatal mortality which has overtaken me. But there is no place of refuge for me and no stronghold to which I may escape. I turn my eyes in every direction, to every place that surrounds me, to the earth's furthermost end. And yet there is no one who can help me now.

---

3 Ecclesiasticus 41:1.

And I hear the grim voice of Death calling to me, sinister, thunderous, and with a hollow spectral resonance, and drawing ever more nigh. It says, "You are mine now! Neither your wealth, nor your honors, nor your reason, nor your knowledge, nor your wisdom, nor friends, nor your kin are able to free you from my clutches! Arise, and let us depart now from the land of the living! For the number of your years and days has been eternally pre-determined by God, and these have reached the appointed end. It is fixed and immutable, and no one—except God alone—has the power to alter it. It is set in the stone of inexorable fate, and the unalterable decree of your passing must now be fulfilled! The wages of sin are death,[4] and these wages must now be paid to you."

O my God (I say to myself), must I really now die? Can this sentence not be revoked or deferred? Must I bid such a hasty farewell to this world, and to the light of day? Alas, how cruel a fiend is Death, how merciless and cold and inexorable!

But, upon hearing this, Death, robed in black and with a sickle in his pallid, emaciated hand, retorts, "Enough of this empty nonsense! Your words cannot

---

4 Romans 6:23.

help you now one iota. Neither your sighs, nor your lamentations, nor your weeping, nor your wailing can gain for you any remission. For soon you shall enter into *my* kingdom, the dreadful realm of shadows and eternal night. And there you will behold and experience such horrors, such bone-chilling abominations as no human eye has ever seen, nor any ear has ever heard, nor the mind of any mortal, even in the state of the most fevered nightmare and mad delirium, has ever imagined!

"But do not protest that this is unfair," continued Death in dreadful and reproachful tones. "For you knew, or should have known, the inevitability and the anguish of this hour. You have had sufficient time to contemplate it and to prepare yourself properly—indeed, you have had your whole life to prepare for this moment!" At this, he laughed sardonically. "I assure that earth shall disappear, the sun shall darken, the heavens themselves shall vanish, before you will be freed from my cold embrace!"

"Alas," I lamented to the skeletal apparition, "how evil and horrid a thing you are, O Death! For you, my ultimate adversary, have come to me uninvited, as an unwelcome and unexpected visitor. And now you wish to drag me off with you to a destination which is entirely unknown to me and to take me to a place where I would rather not go. I am filled with anxiety and dread, for I know that I must now depart from this earthly sphere, but I have no idea where it is that I am going. All I know is that wherever I do go, there I shall remain forever and ever!"

Then, overcome with sorrow and turning my voice to God in humble lament, I cried out, "O God, truly now I see that my mortal life is to pass from me, never to return, and neither shall I see a human being again in the land of the living, nor will I look upon the things of this world again,[5] as I now utter my final farewell!"

---

5 See Isaiah 38:11.

6

A Lament over Time Wasted

[The discourse in the person of a sinner about to die continues.]

And then, as I lay there in the throes of death and fully aware that I had but a few moments left, I reflected upon the time I had wasted during my life. How greatly was this wasted time to be lamented and regretted, these days which I permitted to slip away in vain! How foolishly and profitless did I let my life pass by, wasting it neglectfully and carefully as if it were a thing of no value whatsoever, or as if it were endless in scope and would never run out. I squandered my time like an irresponsible spendthrift squanders money, not considering for a moment that it was both precious and limited!

From my youth, I strayed from the path of God's truth and refused to let the light of righteousness be my guide. Rather, I wore myself out on the highways of iniquity and perdition—and, verily, I was sorely deceived by the temptations of wickedness. For the ways of sin were not ways of delight and pleasure (as I had misguidedly imagined them to be) but rather of difficulty, emptiness, and disappointment. Truly, I was wretched and foolhardy not to have walked in the straight and narrow ways of the Lord!

Alas, what benefit has all my pride and vainglory brought me now? At this moment of my mortal dissolution, what profit have I gained from all my avaricious and insatiable striving after riches and pleasure? For these have all vanished:

> like an insubstantial shadow passing in the night;
> or like a courier or herald who runs by swiftly, without pausing to linger;
> or like a ship hastening through the waves, which leaves not a trace of it passing;
> or like a bird flying through the air, which is quickly gone and leaves no footprint of its flight;
> or like the sound of a bell ringing out, which, once it has ceased to toll, leaves no lasting impression or memory;

> or like an arrow which cuts through the air—once it has gone, the air through which it passed immediately closes in upon itself, and not a trace of it ever having been remains.

My years have been totally consumed in the pursuit of my iniquity! Now both my life and my hope disappear like feathers blown away by a breeze; or like foam of the ocean which is scattered by a gale; or smoke dispersed by the wind; or like the remembrance of a guest who stays for but one day and then is forgotten.[6]

Hence it is that my words are drenched with bitterness, and my reflections are filled with pain. My heart is sorrowful, and my eyes grow dark in melancholy and regret.

Alas, who will grant that I may be restored to the person who I formerly was in days gone by? That I may again wear the garment of strength and energy once more, and regain the beauty and vitality of my younger days? Yes, in those days, I believed that I had a multitude of years ahead of me, and so I felt I could safely ignore all the evils which have now suddenly befallen me!

In those days—the days of my youth and my prime—I cared nothing at all for eternity, nor did I

---

6 See Wisdom 8:5–12.

appreciate the grave perils which surrounded me. And with these perils I flirted all too freely, as if life were a mere game. Yet now I would give the entire world, the entire universe, to gain for myself a single year, a single day, a single extra hour!

And how foolishly I once wasted the precious gift of time, as if it was of no account or of no value! Yes, I drifted like a ship upon the ocean, letting the winds of vanity and waves of vice push me to and fro, entirely careless and oblivious of my final and ultimate destination.

But now, like a fish caught upon a hook, or like a bird trapped in a snare, I am captured by the inescapable grasp of death, the hunter of souls! The time I wasted is gone forever, and the many opportunities of repentance I had are now gone. Would that I could purchase a single hour of full strength and energy in which to confess my sins, and—by penance and contrition—gain God's graces and forgiveness! But, for me, it cannot be.

7

Regrets Concerning the Deferral of Repentance and Reformation

[The discourse in the person of a sinner about to die continues.]

Truly, I am so very sorrowful and so utterly miserable that words cannot suffice to express it! Is it any wonder if my eyes now overflow with tears and sighs of regret issue from the depths of my heart? For I look back upon the moments, days, and years I have let slip by foolishly and realize that these can never ever be called back or reclaimed.

O my God, why was I so negligent, and why did I so improvidently procrastinate thus before coming to true wisdom? Why did I waste my days in useless and inane conversations, in pointless activities, and in empty and futile thoughts—living like one who is in a dream, or who is blindly stupefied with intoxication?

In particular, why did I neglect myself, my conscience, and my soul so? My heart, only now pierced with compunction, weeps with inexpressible regret over the time I wasted so vainly. For I ambitiously desired to know the course of the stars, the movements of the heavens, and the hidden causes of natural phenomena. I aspired to investigate the powers and properties of the different minerals and the customs of other people with avid eagerness. How vainly and fatuously did I study such things, applying myself to them with futile and profitless curiosity! And thus I expended the precious time granted to me by God—and all for what? I came to know many, many things, it is true, but my own self I did not know.

Why ever did I expend so much energy on accumulating vain and useless learning when I did not bother to study that which was truly necessary for me to complete this perilous journey of life and death, and so to arrive safely at my eternal dwelling place? I have learned much about nature, about science, about history, and about literature, but how to live well and how to die well—that which is most essential—I never even troubled myself to study!

And it is for this reason that I am now filled with horror and shudder with nameless trepidation at the solitary pilgrimage upon which I am about to embark—that is to say, the final, longest, and loneliest pilgrimage of death. Yes, in this darksome journey which now confronts me, I shall depart from this familiar sphere of time and space to enter the unknown land of eternity and pass over the threshold through which none may return and cross the somber river of stygian[7] darkness to arrive at the plutonian[8] shores of the beyond.

How carefully and diligently I should have prepared for this moment, counting all efforts devoted to this endeavor to be supremely well spent! Since my future and final fate and the totality of my enduring happiness or my timeless torments depend upon it, it would surely have been wise to have dedicated myself entirely to ensuring my readiness for this solemn and inevitable eventuality. But, alas, in my days of health and vigor, I spared barely a thought, barely a moment, for such matters! In doing this, I became a treacherous traitor

---

7 The adjective derived from the mythical river Styx, which (according to classical mythology) the dead cross to arrive at the underworld.

8 The adjective from the mythical figure of Pluto, the Roman god of the dead, indicating figuratively here complete and dismal darkness.

to my own soul and a deserter of my own salvation. For who has been hurt by my own sins more than my own self?

Oh, I *should* have learned, before anything else, how to die well! Indeed, I sincerely wish to learn even *now*, but time has fled from me, and perhaps it is already too late for me.

But for *you* who read my words and know what my thoughts are as I face my final curtain, for *you* who are still in the flower of your youth and still rejoice in strength and life, yes, for *you*, I say it is not too late! For there is still ample time for good deeds, for walking in the ways of God, and for meriting the healing balm of heaven's mercy through sincere repentance and humble penance! Spend this time, the flower of your life, with the Lord, and undertake to carry His yoke while you still have the strength and vitality to do so. Fill your days with holy occupations, with prayer and reflection! For you will eventually be in the same situation that I am in now when death knocks upon your door. And, alas, this could well be sooner than you expect. Beware lest you end up in the same wretched predicament of regret and fear that I am in!

I recall my own misspent and ill-governed youth, a prey to capricious whims and nefarious impulses. How tightly I was held thrall by the passions and lusts of the flesh, and how proudly did I despise those voices which admonished me for my dissolute ways! Deluded, I imagined my servitude to sin and my slavery to the flesh to be liberty. My ear adamantly refused to hear the wise word of discipline and wisdom, and my heart treated with contempt the kindly counsels of restraint and sobriety. Now, my God, I have fallen into the deepest pit of the shadow of death! In my former pride and erstwhile arrogance, I haughtily scorned the call to repentance. And now my opportunities for amending my life have fled from me, never to return!

The inescapable grasp of death closes in upon me, and every fiber of my being shivers as I feel its cold and ghoulish fingers clutching me. Pain and anguish surround me, and nameless dread assails me on all sides. My heart is torn asunder, every sinew of my body melts, and I am constrained like one bound with heavy chains. I am terrified at my departure hence, and yet I know that I cannot remain for much longer.

How I long to do due penance for my dissipated and godless life, and yet because of my bodily weakness and anguish of mind, I find myself wholly unable to do so fittingly. Fear and panic paralyze my mind and my faculties, like a quail which has been seized in the cruel talons of a falcon, or a dove seized by a rapacious hawk. My concentration and my resolve are rendered powerless and impotent, and are scattered like dust in the wind. There is nothing of which I think about apart from some means of evading death and fleeing from my impending demise. And this I long for desperately, like a rodent trapped in a burning house trying to escape from the searing flames which approach it. But I know in the depths of my heart that it is utterly impossible.

My conscience torments me, and the insidious enemies of my soul—my own vices and sins—surround me like deadly foes, while above me demons hover, like black vultures waiting to take their glut of my soul, the moment my mortal breath expires. Shall it be that cruel death will thus separate me from all my hopes?

8

The Uncertainty of the Last-Minute Repentance and Conversion

[The discourse in the person of a sinner about to die continues.]

How blessed and fortunate are those who arrive opportunely at timely conversion and repentance, and set themselves at rights with God before their allotted span of days has ended: how secure and tranquil will be their departure from this ephemeral world of trials and tribulations!

But, in contrast, the passing of those who leave their attention to ensuring their salvation until their last days is always a wretched experience, dominated by anxiety and uncertainty. For they find themselves longing for an "eleventh hour" repentance. But who knows whether such penitence is really sincere and effective or not? For even the person who is dying cannot really tell whether they are genuinely sorry for their sins, or if they simply fear the fires of hell which otherwise await them. And who can possibly evaluate whether contrition of heart is genuine or sufficient when it is not (and cannot be) accompanied by any corresponding and commensurate deeds? For just as "faith without works is dead,"[9] so are words and intentions which are unsupported by actions.

Woe is me, that I continually put off amending my life and procrastinated in attending to my eternal salvation! Often I formed good intentions and made resolutions to improve—and yet I never put them into effect. Whether this was through sloth, tepidity, complacency, or stubbornness, I cannot truly say.

O tomorrow, tomorrow, false and lying tomorrow! You have deceived me, and I have allowed myself to be deceived. For by depending upon you, O illusive and illusionary tomorrow, I have permitted myself to be engulfed in the abyss of death! For you have abandoned me and fled from me; yes, to me there will be no more tomorrow.

---

[9] James 2:26.

And what response will I give when dragged before the strict tribunal of Final Judgment? When I look back on my life, can I find one single day which I have devoted entirely to the service of the Lord? Can I find one single hour which I have dedicated completely to fulfilling the will of my Creator?

O my God, I shall stand before You and before all the saints confused and embarrassed, anxiously awaiting my eternal sentence. For all of the secrets of my heart and all the wicked machinations of my mind will be exposed to the sight of all. And I shall be called upon to give an account or explanation of each one of my sins and failings, in both what I have done and what I have failed to do. And there will be no place for specious excuses, nor any opportunity to deny my manifest and self-evident guilt. O Lord, what will I say then, and what will I do? From where shall come my help if not from Your unmerited mercy alone?

Now, O Reader, the time when I shall be confronted by this dreaded tribunal of judgment draws nigh for me! This world, in which I had expected to remain for so much longer, now flees from me; presently, it shall disappear entirely, like a passing dream from which one awakes.

My friends, listen to me now carefully, I implore you! Know that at this moment, I would rejoice more for one of you to say a single Hail Mary for the salvation of my poor soul than I would to receive an infinite treasure of gold and silver, or to be granted sovereignty over all the kingdoms of earth.

9

The Unreliability of Human Assistance in the Hour of Death

[The discourse in the person of a sinner about to die continues.]

Oh, how deceitful are the crowds of so-called friends which congregate around the dying, and how deceptive are the honeyed words of physicians! For they all promised good things to me, and all confidently assured me of my recovery. "There is absolutely nothing to fear," they told me, "and you are in no peril at all. No need to rush to make your confession to a priest! This malady is nothing but a temporary ailment and a minor vexation of the nerves, which will cure itself in due course. Simply rest and take things easy, and put all anxiety from your mind, for this infirmity will soon pass!"

O my false friends (or rather, true enemies!), by following your guidance and counsel and not admitting the reality of my impending death, I was defrauded of the opportunity of timely repentance and reconciliation. How I regret paying heed to your consoling but misleading assurances!

It was not long ago that when I looked upon my own body, I saw it full of life and strength, and abloom with the flower of youth. But now I behold it dry and desiccated, its former glory gone like the flower of the field, which springs up in the morning and withers by the end of the day.[10]

Alas, where have all those things gone in which I once so confidently placed my hopes and my trust? What has become of my youthful liberty and carefree nonchalance, my prosperity and success, and my robust health and strength?

But you, O Death, now laugh at me and mock me, as I recognize that all along I was in your power and in your thrall, even in the midst of apparent life and health. And it is only fitting that you have come upon me unexpectedly, since for all my life I refused to prepare myself for your fatal visit!

---

[10] See Isaiah 40:6–8.

And now the hour of my final dissolution approaches, and my mortal life draws to its termination.

My vision fails,
My skin grows pale,
My hair is gray,
Life ebbs away.
My spirits leave me,
My hopes deceive me;
This day's my last,
My time has passed.

Yes, my time in this earthly realm has reached its end, and now my soul prepares to depart for the invisible and unfathomable domains of the "great beyond." Time will be exchanged for eternity, light exchanged for everlasting darkness, motion for unchanging and implacable stillness. The hour of inescapable judgment awaits me when the omnipotent King shall pronounce His irrevocable and unalterable sentence!

My eyes overflow with an unstoppable stream of bitter tears. Yet are these the precious tears of genuine compunction, or merely the commonplace tears of fear, anxiety, and regret? And do my lamentations profit me at all in this, my final hour?

But, lo, a grim shadow now casts its hideous darkness upon me, and the cold fingers of mortality tighten palpably around my quaking heart! Death, my final adversary, my companion who has accompanied me, unseen, throughout my entire earthly life, has come to take me away forever.

10

A Final Exhortation to Those Who Still Live

[The discourse in the person of a sinner about to die continues.]

Oh, you my friends who read these words, to you I bid my final farewells, just as now I say good-bye also to earthly life itself and the entire realm of time and space. My hands grow cold and my feet are chilled; my face is suffused with the ghastly pallor of the grave, and my vision and senses become faint and confused. My pulse is irregular and weak, and my breathing laborious and shallow. Little by little, my human body is transforming itself into the horror of a corpse, before it returns to the dust and ashes from whence the omnipotent hand of God once formed it.

And while all this is happening, those standing around me continue to say, "Oh Brother, keep your hopes up! Do not be dejected or depressed, for you still have a very good chance!" Alas, little do they know, or how little are they prepared to admit! For many years, I went astray to pursue the paths of worldliness and wickedness, neglecting the well-being of my soul to seek the pleasures of the flesh and the vanities of the heart. Will these last few moments of regret and sorrow suffice to restore me to the path of eternal beatitude and to atone for the sins of an entire lifetime? God alone knows.

For I realize that whatever state my conscience is in when I leave this world, in that same state it will accompany me when I appear before the divine tribunal of judgment. My own conscience, exposed to the view of all, will serve there as the principal evidence and witness, either for or against me. And this, in turn, will determine my everlasting destiny!

Blessed indeed are those who keep this moment of death before the eyes of the mind every moment of their lives. For they shall direct all their actions according to the final end to which they aspire—that is to say, safe entrance into the kingdom of heaven. They will arrive at this point in security, peace, and tranquility, and, indeed, even with joy and relief.

But as for me, I know full well that this night is to be my last. By tomorrow morning, I ask you, where do you think my poor spirit will be dwelling, and in what realm shall my immortal soul abide? Will it be dwelling in the celestial fields of eternal light and ineffable beauty, accompanied by the glorious hosts of angels and the wondrous communion of saints? Or will it rather be groaning in the infernal abyss of nameless darkness, where the fire is never extinguished and the worm does not cease to gnaw,[11] tormented by hideous demons and the grim specters of the wretched damned?

To whom will I turn in this, my hour of desperation? O Lord, my God, You proclaim Yourself to be merciful, and indeed You are very truly so. *You* will be my leader and my way in this dark exodus which I am shortly to undertake! You will be my refuge and the portal through which I may escape the infinitude of woes which besieges me.

As I look around me, my eyes perceive the terrestrial light of this mortal life but dimly now, and yet I seem to behold the spiritual reality of the world beyond this

[11] See Mark 9:48.

one. And there are swarms of demons hovering above my body, eagerly waiting to seize my soul. O Lord, how terrible and frightful is their aspect—these malevolent demons who long for nothing so much as to take the spiritual spark of my being away to the realms of chaos and eternal night, and to make it a companion to their own unspeakable miseries! Do not forget, O God, that this is the same soul which You created in Your own image, for no other purpose than to praise You forever and ever and to partake in Your own infinite glory and bliss. Lord, remember that I am Your child (albeit a wayward one), and do not abandon me to everlasting perdition.

Good-bye, my friends and my beloved readers. I myself now depart to stand before the inexorable throne of God's judgment, to return an account of all my thoughts, actions, and words—yes, all that I have done and all that I have failed to do. May your kind prayers help my soul to obtain mercy and pardon for my sinful life, through the grace of Christ and the power of His most precious blood. And may the Blessed Virgin Mary, the radiant choirs of holy angels, and the glorious communion of saints all supplicate and plead for my salvation, though I am entirely unworthy of their advocacy—for God knows how very much I am in need of it!

As for yourselves, I urge you with the utmost fervor to learn both to live and to die well in the Lord, while you still have the time and opportunity. For in God alone is our hope, our salvation, and our eternal life. Let us earnestly pray for each other so that we may all find peace, pardon, and everlasting happiness, with Him who lives and reigns forever and ever! Amen.

G. Doré

Part III
Canticles to Heaven

11

A Canticle on the Joys of Heaven and the Choirs of Angels

How great the joy, what sweet delights,
Which shall abound in heaven's heights!
There Christ the Lord and Mary mild,
Bestow, in grace, peace undefiled.

In palaces of azure[1] cloud,
The angel hosts give voice to loud
Eternal hymns, in countless choirs,
With all the joy which love inspires.

Their hearts enrapt in waves of bliss,
Receiving God's most holy kiss.

---

[1] A shade of bright blue.

On lyric harp and crystal flute
And silver shawm[2] and gold-strung lute,

They resonate a rhapsody
Of glory to the Trinity.
They lithely fly on mystic wing,
In honeyed voice their hymns to sing.

Acclaim they thus in tones sublime,
"Thrice-holy God, O King divine!"
And in that realm, no pain abides,
Nor mourning lurks, nor sorrow hides.

The seraphim, in awe, adore;
through light-filled vaults, they fleetly soar.
And cherubim, on bended knee,
Give glory to God's majesty.

Then come the Thrones, Dominions, Powers,
And Virtues next, whose splendor towers,
With vibrant glow and roaring thunder,
Resounding in celestial wonder.

Come Princes next, archangels bright,
Then angel hosts, in dove-winged flight.
In heaven's court they contemplate

---

2 A kind of trumpet-like wind instrument with a powerful tone, which angels are traditionally often depicted as playing.

God's holy face, His marvels great.
On earth below, they watch and guide,
As gentle guards, walk by our side.

O star-girt realm of bliss supreme,
Be thou our hope, be thou our dream!
In thy vast halls, O city blest,
Is untold peace, high heaven's rest.
There shines pure light ineffably,
And souls exult, forever free.

To God alone be homage paid,
Whose wondrous love such things has made!

12

A Canticle to the Angels and Saints in Heaven

O citizens of heaven,
And angels, lend your ear;
O, listen to our pleadings,
Our supplications hear!

While in this woeful valley,
We cry and we lament,
As to the hall supernal[3]
Our tears and sighs are sent.

O, raise us when we stumble,
Give succor[4] when we fall!
Look down on us in mercy,
And hear each desperate call.

---

3 Celestial, or heavenly.

4 Help or assistance.

The holy saints and angels
Exult in purest light,
But we, the seed of Adam,
Must wander through sin's night.

The soul inflamed by God's love
A grievous burden bears—
It sees not its Beloved,
Amidst telluric[5] cares.

It walks by faith, and trusting
In God's protecting grace,
To lead it to the heavens
To gaze on Christ's sweet face.

O, Faith and Hope together,
With Sister Charity,
Exclaim, "Beloved Savior,
O, lead us unto thee!"

From heaven Jesus answers,
"O Soul, weep not nor cry,
When mortal trials are ended,
To my embrace thou'll fly,

---

[5] Earthly.

"As I to meet my Father
Before thee ere[6] have flown,
To send to thee the Spirit,
By whom all truth is shown.

"But now with hope affixed on
Cerulean[7] gleams above,
Rejoice, anticipating
The fullness of God's love."

For death is but a portal
To heaven's sweet embrace,
Where we'll rejoice forever,
Exulting in God's grace!

---

6 Already, previously.

7 A shade of blue, characteristic of the color of distant skies.